The Wish Furnace

Randy Blythe

FUTURECYCLE PRESS
www.futurecycle.org

Cover art and design by Chris Lawson and Mike Dolinger; author photo by B. R. Tytler; interior design by Diane Kistner; Minion Pro text and DIN titling

Library of Congress Control Number: 2022951030

Published by FutureCycle Press
Athens, Georgia, USA

ISBN 978-1-952593-48-2

For Bridget

Contents

I

II

III

And what, monks, is the all that is burning?

—The Buddha, from *The Fire Sermon*

I went down, down, down,
And the flames went higher.

—June Carter and Merle Kilgore

You fought hard and you saved and learned,
But all of it's going to burn.

—Arthur Brown

I

Athwart

Crimsoner for spring fights,
cock cardinal darts up,

claims air above the blueberry bush.
Point settled, adamant,

and back down proud,
never unsure of nature's nature.

How many times
will you drop what's in hand

to pick it up again, shoo a wren
from the porch with a broom,

clean mud from soles,
heft river stones rounded

and patient
a thousand years?

Oceans of sweat over what
falls away anyway.

So many souls brow-furrowed
over what worse than this

might swing into view.
The teeth of a wish

smile at the taste of juice and pulp
until the tongue finds a seed.

Daddy's Bait

If I'd lived in the Florentine scheme
instead of being a 12-year-old from Alabama,
I might have treated insect souls worse—
penned them in rings where they'd clamber over each other,
smeared with shit and dodging fire—

but this little homemade box
set just inside the camp house door,
wood-framed, wire-meshed, 1' x 1' x 1',
was enough *Inferno* for crickets
doomed to wait for a fishhook through the gut

and enough to make me puzzle over
where to move the hellacious chirruping
so I could sleep at least
part of a May night in Etowah County.

Not outside on the blackberry-winter porch
where I feared half might die of exposure before morning,
trapped in the open, so to say,

so I thought to put them in the next room of the shack
I slept in some nights, on the empty bed,
and we'd huzz to sleep in tandem.

But a half hour later,
my eyes grown itchy at a scraping of legs,
I changed my mind, took the bait
in hand and outside, released
and returned them to grace after all,

left them to find their own warmth in the early greening.
Latch hook lifted, seeing my father's wrath unlocked
at losing his power to let things die
made the risk worthwhile.

History of the Absent

Unseen in the corner of the eye,
you come to into nothing,

like a useless wish,

like a diaphanous Madeline
in another room,

like an empty assumption
drifting above a canyon of thought-

lessness—a slo-mo Knievel
who never reaches the other ramp.

Use forgiveness
to outwit sins of omission,

pass up the chance to practice avoidance,

celebrate with silence,

fail, after numerous canceled attempts,
to make it onto the secret society's agenda,

make nothing of a blank expression,

miss the committee meeting
in the parlor, just before the Gestapo arrive,

forget to lament not having lamented,

never know you can never know.

The Ten Thousand Names of Dog

Unlike saving a glom treasure
for some future chomp

in the shade, humans bury
bones of the unsaid in smiles or silence

or worse, whole regiments of secrets
that grow, with time, undiggable

since packed earth
dries like concrete—solid,

inscrutable, too occult
for weak wishes.

Environing the near pond,
fishes and frogs,

if they could, would murmur,
attribute attribute attribute.

Once a year, the water
tries to burble a word

that seems apt, but air
shuts down the first syllable.

If you didn't know better,
you'd think that to trot by

nonchalantly on that day,
genitals asway, would be

to dismiss the very gift, to ignore
the nose's effort to have you notice

an uncomfortable odor somewhere
near the bottom of your sneaker.

Ishmael

Stillness from a sigh.
        The look
of knowing and being known
           that has just disappeared
from an eye.
        A whitening film
in its place.

        Below misted air still
alive enough to make daylight
        rainbows,
the calm at the end of the chase
        won't let me ignore
fellow-feeling: scenes
        too crimson-soaked to slip
through the sieve of days
        unheeded.

No other way
        to make the sea
this kind of reverent,
        and why I have to face
my own refusal to see
        when the spout's huffing
dies away
        and the silence
lays claim.

        As an angel
to the Lord,
        no matter which way
earth turns,
        so this giant eye
gazes sunward in death,
        its end with God,
not His pretenders.

Klook

(Kenny Clarke—1/9/1914-1/26/1985)

You'd need a music about
getting loose, losing,
feening, making kicks—
since coming home was to a war
against a different bunch of Nazis.

Kicks to kick, get kicks, and get kicked by.
You could raise your hand
like you needed to say something
or needed something to say,
but you couldn't see it in the dark
and it looked like neither could anybody else.

You stay kicked in the chest because
when you're a drowning croaker fish
without a slicker in 4:00 a.m. rain,
hanging onto the back of a city truck,
you don't believe you're much. And nobody
said there had to be an earthquake
in a bunch of black folks moving
over the water again for something better.

To go after some kicks
is at least to make your own way to die—
in the gravel, in a fix, in a car,
and a way or two the other way,
like Paris or between somebody's legs.

Back away. Feather the big drum,
move the right hand uptown, to the ride.
Park your left hand on a nice curve
and kick your boot pedal up Utah beach.
You're cutting time, but you're not
waiting around for anybody to fall.
Good bombs go off when you
put your foot down where you are.

Darrell, Suppertime

You're still mostly there in your mind
    in my memory of sixty years ago,

minus, for the moment, the wad of Bloodhound plug
    you'd spit out before a meal,

tractor-eyed, overall-clad, boot-scuffed, dusty,
wrung out and hungry come summer evenings,

fork-stabbing the best quarter of a late tomato
    the way you always did,

as suddenly sharp in demeanor
as the tomato was in taste,
    which itself couldn't get more acidic
    when Dog Days came, when Rutgers
    ripened smaller than a plum
    and could pucker a mouth dry.

As quick to find fault as any self-respecting dirt farmer—
with a tomato, a hoe handle, or somebody's character—
    since surviving had been all that mattered,

and quick in another way,
with the razor strop, Daddy said, when the laziest of your
    crop of children slowed finishing out the row.

***

Old hand at too much sun and wizening
    and creaking your weak back out of bed
    at daylight again, you stayed
    red-grizzled and ruddy-faced,
    tobacco drool escaping down your chin most days,
your body grown numb to living
    in that way too many days in the cottonfield
    can bring, when just getting enough
    to be able to eat reasonable and buy boots once a year
keeps attention drifting to the horizon.

With decades, you grew interested in being
    neither *there* nor *not there*
      since presence of mind was not as much an issue
      for a man who got the job done
      for the sake of food and little bellies.

Not a happy or sad man by the time I knew you
in your seventh decade,
    just a man not entirely accepting
    of what you thought the Good Lord had given,
because silence was all you had
    when the heat of any July day in Etowah county
    melted all but the barest wherewithal away

and you'd push yourself past pushing yourself
to reach the hellish calm of acceptance—
    not because it was preferred
    or some bullshit about God's will,
but because the resolve of generations
    said, "This is your measure."

And you'd long since become heedless enough
of anything divine, as time passed,
    and took up the habit of staying home Sundays
    while she and all five trooped off to Macedonia Baptist
    snazzed up in their spitshines and flour sacks
and you could go spend some quiet time with the bottle
    you had hidden in the feed barrel in the barn.

***

Fork in your off hand, tines down,
    index finger crooked atop
    and guiding the fork over oilcloth flowers,
    your mouth way past any smirk of resentment
    since you'd lived a life so far down in work
    there could be nothing else—
you could be made of nothing else—
you'd point shakily at the serving platter
like an old man at a crosswalk
    wagging his crooked finger
    at a punk in a Dodge.

A wordless eater like all our family,
hunched and circling your plate with your arms
(while she hovered, never sitting down to eat with us,
waiting till we finished, to sit alone
and eat cold leftovers),
you'd make a meal of it, sour-seeming
        at the business of sustenance,
        poking at your share of the provender
        with a planter's stare,
        dourly smacking at sweet corn, green beans,
        mashed potatoes, oven-fried chicken,

a man who'd made his way, who'd run
        a family like a tractor till it quit on him,
        and all five grew up and out—
        off to war or marriage—
        and there wasn't anything left to fix,

just an aging man ignoring the beginnings of the dementia
that would ripen in your head for fifteen years,
        not knowing you were pointing that finger
        toward the day you'd be lost to everybody
including yourself.

Sami Painting

Moose upside down wants
snow to touch him and make the sky
as wide as sunlight.

For this desire it's said
there are nine names,
for snow twenty-three, for sunlight one,

for Moose a season of flakes.
Houses and people are still
houses and people. A man

with a hemlock twig claims horizon.
Everything but meaning returns.
Meaning cannot be eaten,

not even gnawed, says Beaver.
Beaver is Moose small with big teeth
but no antlers.

Night's houses have teeth,
but in the day their mouths are closed.
You cannot fold up sunlight

because it's not paper.
The sun is happy this is so,
so is all day.

Elvis Dives

Freeze the home movie; it's 1968
in Graceland's side yard, and he's about
to leap between heaven and Memphis,

the J. C. Penney plaid trunks
girdling the boy-like ungainliness
of a diver self-taught at best. He knows he's got

nothing on the perfect jackknife
new-mom Priscilla performed a minute ago.
How fine the world was

before the Comeback Tour took its toll,
how sanguine even
the peskiest friend with an 8mm camera—

as well-meaning as Tennessee.
As if there were no Tet, no Kennedys,
no other King to stride

to his balcony, this royalty seems
doubt-free and meant for its own Camelot.
All languid big hair and sunlight

in the poolside chaise lounge,
Priscilla smiles, watching him in a rare moment
when his cocksureness seems to have failed him—

no coiffed snarl in sunglasses this time.
A plowboy nearing the creek,
he has slue-footed down the board

and sprung head ass feet sprawl first
into an apogee frozen in the lens,
mid-flail, gravity postponed forever.

As If It Were

Do you at least get to choose?
    Ibex? Oryx? Gazelle?

You're stuck proverbially somewhere between horns
    until you no longer are.
    At that point, sharp as it will be,
    there will be no point.

What gall that genes chose to worry this wound
    long before there was a you.

As if knowing anything, especially that there's an end,
    puts you at an advantage.
    What a gift, considering.

As if anticipating
    the last scene you live toward
    could make you matter more.

Try to measure that matter:
    the measure that's supposed to matter
    until you find
    it's the matter measure won't gauge.
    And what if it did?

With that gift of evolution, play all the angles,
    trying as if you could get beyond your
    fooling-yourself-that-you're-awake awakeness,

as if breath number forty thousand
    six hundred and fourteen
    in a given week makes more sense.

As if it were the one that made a difference.

Initiation

In a county of dust and freckle-red faces,
a boy stands in his past,
under a tall pecan tree,
shouldering a Daisy pump with a bent barrel,
waiting for anything to land.

Inside the dear nearby old house are family
and a day's concerns: tomatoes to peel,
hallways to scurry through, cabinets to reach into.

He is outside, zeroed in on the task.
In that moment, he's a twelve-year-old,
his inner life composed of
equal parts patience and frustration.

The boy doesn't see past his aim,
has little save a vague sense
of the millions of thoughtlets of increasing weight
that will play out his future.

When the cream-soft mother dove
flutters as she lights in a crotch of the tree,
something in him believes she has fallen
into his world. He shoots

and realizes, surprised, that he's hit her,
crooked barrel and all,
and that she will squat there for a time,
no longer able to rise,
claws clinging to life,
while his childhood flies away.

Dixieland

(for the Guys and Dolls)

Eddie gets wayward in his measures,
notes reedy and thin as his hair,
slowing us and the song to a sputter.
He's old, and we believe him,
but his beat-up clarinet warms the room,
dim notes and all,
and the rest of us fall in with the soft fire
the seasoned muster on a good day:

Marion hooting into the tuba,
ham-handed Al plinking along on the tenor,
Clyde plinking too, rolling his eyes at Marion,
George just back from his second mild stroke,
horn at the ready—like we could
put down our instruments
and best intentions and walk away
and the tune would continue,
way down yonder despite us,
the whole assisted-living cafeteria
transported to the riverbank at dusk,
rocking to the calliope downstream.

I tap-dance my stick tips along the snare rim
when Jim hits stride, his last note clear
with a buttery touch of Bubber Miley
through his band-teacher's decorum;
Rex's trombone dovetails in with a growl
rank as a storm drain—
Carmen's tinkling keys the rain—
till the next bent note in his dented slide
reaches for the wheelchaired
woman in the front row.
Smiling through his embouchure,
he gives her the big-eye like he hasn't given
and she hasn't seen in seventy years.

As Below

The Lord will never take His foot off the big snake.
So He tells himself. The Lord's sure
some of His symbols need to behave better.

He believes that if He
doesn't believe in the dozens of hatchlings
already coursing through His One Embodyless Body,

crawling up His leg,
swimming sperm-like in the Godhead zygote,
there will be no more worry with snakes of any kind,

even snakes of the mind. So He tells himself.
So He thinks He will not allow the big snake
(you know the one) back into the tree

even if the snake belongs there.
He doesn't want Eve
to become the mother of tomfoolery

and begin to think, "I belong to this tree,
and it belongs to me,
and this fruit is the proof."

Father of all slitherers,
the big snake is a savvy one.
He intends to sneak out from undersandal

in one of those moments of inattention
that plague even the Boss.
He intends to slip his way into a Holy Orifice,

end up in the cockpit behind the Big Eyes,
and if that goes well
look for some kind of switch.

The Summer of My Father's 86th Year and My 56th

It takes not so much anymore
to lean back with my arms up
and smell like Darrell,
alive now only in that
and maybe a hoe's fine edge.
I said the numbers,
then my grandfather's name.
"What?" Daddy said.
Dusk smelling like cattle again,
cicada crosscuts playing out again.
Not so hard now to cheer on the deer tick
at having set her rumpled forehead in me,
her instinct and wisdom without conceit,
the dignity of the humble and inevitable,
the latitudes and longitudes
of a blind drive to feed,
the bliss of the oblivious,
work to be done,
going till wherewithal goes.

Abide

Slo-gro vines
		make for the last of summer—
purple martins' homes in the making,
		gourds to be hollowed out
		and raised on poles.

This tumble clambers over last winter's
		leftover woodpile:
cone-shaped leaves the size of a fuel funnel,
		waiting for relief,
		look up through the dry spell;

the summergreen creep drapes
		over woodpile tarp,
		over cast-over plastic chair,
		over cures of oak and poplar
to blossom into white-bloom paintbrushes—
		vine-end tendril joys,
		secretive fruits below.

By the corn crib,
		a sun-touched sister vine
sprouts newborn buds
		that shy back until they bulb
and hang down from the bars of an old calf feeder
		like a bull cod turned green,
		only, instead of from a belly,
they dangle from a frame of weedgrown rust

and hide from view
		until I walk by one August evening
		and they jump into my notice
		as if they beg
		to tell the story of next March,
		the return of swift aces,
and how being emptied
		leads to being borne up.

Death in the South

At effort's end we lie down
      in a dank corner of the century,
when the mockingbird is silent
      and the dog star nods,

all us slue-footed, overall-clad,
      runny-nosed kids, muddy-faced and laughing
but alert near shrill voices and switch bushes,
      all us women wary of the whims

of whiskey-breathed men
      but drawn to talk, through a haze of cicadas,
of pole beans and church pantries,
      all us officers of various societies

with blue stares sharp as straight razors
      and way too much hard wind
pushing us down the street,
      carnations flying off our lapels,

all us great-grandchildren of slaves and sharecroppers
      bound for the great democracy of the spirit
but still deep-down suspicious of everything
      but a box, a plot, a big stone angel

leaning over there over the boss.
      In a lesser-known
precinct of eternity, a big sweaty county
      where summer can sparkle like the grace of God,

knowing we deserve an end,
      we'll turn toward the dark
with a wish to rejoin the millions of children
      who never got to be cousin Boyd or Nanette,

who too soon forever were made to share
      the glory of the ground
under churchyards now full of lamb-heavy tombstones
      grown mossy and stoic in the rain.

Readiness

It's impossible to say exactly
what grackles do by the hundreds,
collecting craw-grist and themselves
in the bustle before fall.

Quiet as black ghosts, except for a dry rustle
and the stray self-naming call,
they shift oak leaves until
a brief flutter is raised *en masse,*

like eager, neuralgic monks among stacks
from which one sweet booksecret of this life
or the next might be gobbled—
the risks of sultry updrafts

or the Thicket to end all thickets.
Underneath the busyness
is persistence so wild it's demonic,
patterns of pecking within a ground-grid

(as if each bird knows its space),
ornithological ordinances stuck-to
to the last unlucky mite
until, when the sentry clicks danger

at a shoe shifting on concrete,
the time comes to rise
in a ballet of fractal motion,
a dark-matter mirror reflecting

upswept density, loose unison,
swooping arcs full of emptiness,
as loyal to season's end
as a waving hand is to a body.

II

Those Many Years

The tremor in his voice,
his eyes, his playing,
the actor playing Sam singing

"just a sigh" softly enough
to bring Ilsa to the point of tears,

the scene about more, you'd think,
than old Dooley Wilson
playing upright and sympathetic

and again on command
because he'd been given little choice as an actor,

the pay was good enough,
and nobody else could downplay grief
like the dark-skinned friend

who understood self-torture
in ways Rick wouldn't know himself,

acting a comfort to our comfortless
and courageous hero who would
put her and her kisses

and the matter-of-factness of sacrifice
on a plane and watch it fly away.

Ricky

Mean as hyenas, we'd yell,
"Hold up at third, Holcomb,"
      faking concern the way seventh graders can
      in the middle of a prank.

Instead, a *petit mal* quiver, you slowed
      to a halt between second and third,
your arms still running,
mind blinked those seconds it took
      Del to make the throw from right
      and Bill to tag you, stand back,
      and point cackling with the rest of us.

In the game I would have played
      if I'd had any idea of the big score,
I drop my mask and mitt on the plate
      and walk to where you stand on the base line.

Up close, the breath from your acne-ravaged face
      drowns out the catcalls from around the diamond.
I take the hand, knuckle-scarred
      from too many post-seizure fights,
      and lead you around third—
Now, Ricky, Now! Run!—in sight of home.

For the first time I see the pockmarked cheeks,
the eyes rolled back and staring at the white paint
      on the ceiling of your skull,
      lids half-open and fluttering,
      head stuck bobbing a silent *Yes.*

Instinct

If you behave like a wasp,
God will broom you down
since, if you were a wasp,
you'd only know
how to behave like a wasp
and not like a human behaving
like one, so you wouldn't know
that to build a spit-paper nest
on God's back porch
is a bad move. Every ounce
of wherewithal you have
told you to build there,
and it was the very
wherewithal God installed.

So you already know
the situation is strange,
you're already pretending
the sky is a mirror,
and you can't not stare up.
There's no fun in realizing
you can only be here.
Next thing you're moving 10-ton
blue or porphyry stones 150 miles upriver.
You're carving
giant poses into a mountain.
You don't know
foolishness from ambition.
You're brewing twisted tales
in exasperation tea
because you're sure
there are mysteries in your cup.
Then the blind man
comes to your back door
selling brooms.

Given the Point

IT'S GOING RAIN DOWN FIRE is
black spray-painted on the wall
   of the Fifth Avenue tunnel entrance,
the downtown-apocalypse graffitist
   maybe too God-addled for *"TO."*

Baffled by the cipher prophecy can become,
   especially when it's incomplete,
the passing reader can shrug his shoulders up.
   Which, on driving by, one might do
at most any graffiti, open-palmed, eyes a-roll.

   Which is quite unlike worms on the sidewalk,
who can only shrug sideways
   when it rains down rain
even though they're as desperate
   as anybody would be to get out from under
and find higher ground.

   The body's final acquaintances,
worms have power
   unnoticed until too late,
while walkers-above,
   spray-painters-on-walls
and shruggers at apocalypse,
   assume worms are good for little.
Aeration. Fish bait.

   Worms squirm through their mealy lives,
are sticky and too busy coupling and working dirt
   to convey end-time urgency, we assume,

while we ponder what's left out,
   why somebody would write on a wall,
what if anything the message could mean,
   where to go if not through the tunnel.

Old Hurt

New pain is
a fresh walnut; crack
into the bitter black
till the kernel appears:

relief ready to extract,
eye, palate, aliment, crisp and easy

compared to the wounds
you were hoping would heal over,

for which one metaphor won't suffice—
worn dull, not shiny, having logged
much spin time, long past best shape—

a troupe of neuralgias
waiting for the season closer
and its celebration of the honor of aging.

If you could see
the other side of the wall
you're heading toward

(one might call it late middle age;
another, a memory that got stuck),

you'd find trees, ducks,
benches, maybe water.

Further down the path,
past feigned sagedom,
there's incontestable proof,

in direr trials that come
when stamina wanes,

that the "kill" part's moot,
and the "make stronger" part
is for a fresher fool.

Signoff

No more dark outside
in the dark wanting in,
no bulb light inside yellow rooms

lit shining alone in the shack-light
or pointing yellow fingers out the window,
accusing the field-dark,

woods-dark, no-moon-dark
of keeping secrets.
No more half-hearted assent.

No argument. No need for consent.
No more trumpet flowers'
orange silence, iced tea in the shed

while the afternoon takes a shower,
new-mown scent
reaching a hand into memory.

No staring at the sky,
chips for shoulders,
karma boomerangs of lavender or turd.

No more climbing up life stairs
in hope of afterlife stars, no more fear of
dirt as final home, no more

cathedral of red-flow, chill
caught in sadness, thrill in transgression,
hopes lit or abandoned,

looking in someone's eyes to live,
me to think of as me, us to think of.
Us to think. Us.

The Buddha Unsays

Made sound, his discerning
could be fish hawk or muskrat,

could ripple out and ring
with or without a bell.

Lotus along the stream
of aftermind, he nods,

We are burning.
Every thing that is

knows he knows
that, from the bottom of

a furnace of wishes,
the reach up or out is for a hand

that seems to be there.
And those he eyes,

blinking, hoping themselves
worthy of the right water,

cannot leave the pretty fire alone.
For the fevered, banished

inside their own round,
to cry "Unfair!"

carries no relief.
And this One before

and again inhabits a need
not to shape back into word,

not to reel in, reason with,
or pretend to understand.

Faith

To swifts—flesh and feather
from the summer chimney—

go mosquito spoils
before the evening storm,

under breaking cumulus
and too many grays to name,

when wind is intent, thumbing
through its own whims,

and flights of chittering aeronauts
bank on the unseen.

Imprint

I flip through now and then to this woodcut
      full of the silent panic of the scene in Bethany
      transformed, by Dürer's medium,
into static black and white

with kneeling disciples' and onlookers' faces
      all turned up, as if someone had noticed
      and shared the news
that an orchard's apples were turning.

Clouds, Christ's feet, and the bottom folds of a robe
      are all the artist wants us to see
      above the upturned human eyes.
      No glow around the holy head.
      No sadly knowing downlook.
No scars from thorn, spear, spike.

What would you do in the street
      if you came upon a clot of people
      staring up at the bottoms of a man's feet
      hanging in the air, still close enough
      that they looked almost touchable?
      Would you look for calluses, bunions?
Do a double take at the longer second toe?

Feet dangle under the body being swallowed in the low clouds
      as if, grown most intimate with the dust
      and mud of Galilee's roads
      and the mission of making grace tangible,
they should be the last taken up,

the pedestrian become miraculous,
      imposing on these people's minds
      an image so sudden it'll startle them
      into carrying what they've seen
for the rest of their lives.

Because, having seen it, they will no longer idly wonder
      what anyone, including that man,
could look like floating up into the sky.

To the Task

There are those who say
that, after all his suffering,
Job's questions were so tough
they silenced God,

and that's why
we listen so hard,
as if the long pause
has grown more pregnant.

Was God shut up
the way the Dog Star
shuts up mockingbirds in July?

Divine shame
at a just man's indignation?

Is that why miracles grew vaguer,
more timid?

                              ***

Now God seems baffled,
reluctant at what to do with all that
timelessness.

Sits in the top of a cedar
stretching His wings, preening,
shaping His beak
around weighty silence,

tongue distended,
a little embarrassed
at the outcome of His own paternity.

Stretches finger-feathers
into first one realm then another,
a little uncomfortably,

perhaps shrugging a bit,
always trying for a fit,

like a funeral director
who points his employees to their work,
purses his lips,
adjusts his new suit coat
while the coffin is closed.

Surrection

Like oak, sycamore, hickory, ash
     that steam up out of the ground
in their time,
     in and above dirt and years,
as if they know both sky
     and earth are home,

I'd rather a released soul—
     if there is such a thing—
take a last sip of air before rising
     and be tipsy from the cordial,
uneasy in ascent,
     neither cocksure nor crow-fly,
not up a rail-straight God beam
     like some stained-glass dove
thrown in reverse.

     She sights a new home
but wants to stay where she knows
     and, in that second
rising and reluctance
     tremble together, mirage-like,
in afterblur in and beside the body,
     as if lingering in two places
were an option.

     But as wavering gives way
to a *tremendum* quaver—
     seen and unseen one—
something like heat
     (alive, I hope, with cicadas)
quakes her nearer eternity
     and, free of an earth-long prison,
she makes gravity a lie.

On Earth

"I see men as trees walking,"
the man said.

Jesus resumed rubbing
grit and saliva into his eyes.

Was it because there was more to be seen?
Because not enough was known?

Because to see men as trees walking
is to see men as more than men walking?

To see men as trees walking
is to see feet as roots,

arms as branches, mouth and navel as knots—
a seeing a god-in-man might want to confirm

since getting somewhere one is presently not
does not need to be about legs.

Reason, from that other point of view,
for Jesus to finish rubbing the man's eyes,

for the blind man to find himself
near a completer seeing,

for there to be little difference
between the paths of people and trees.

Blank Is the New Blank

Umpty years of nicks on the stick,
ticks on the tock,
neglect of minute-by-offhand-minute
because, cull it down to white noise,
and the keyboard's nothing but hyphens.

This unmeasurable this
is measured in pain or pleasure,
in busting or getting a nut
under sway of some moldering instinct,
some species-specific amnesia.

More in- and output are needed,
more lives for the unlearning.
Choices are made, it seems,
in the bushes over by the picnic.
But the ants have always staged that
(shhhh, don't let on).

As breath comes and goes
along with every goddamn/
blessed second, a need might arise to resolve—
fueled by the thump in the chest
and the whitest white knuckles musterable—
to improve upon a moment.

At what all know or
under Thine eyes think they do,
then, O Harlequin of Determining,
grant Thee upon them the
exact weight of presumption.

Wild Dogs

These aren't hyenas or jackals
    or even the Serengeti trotters,
whose low motley looks wildebeests dread,
    in the corners of their eyes.

Progeny of Aunt Lou's retriever,
    Uncle Sim's best shepherd,
and others muttying up the mix,
    these rounders bring home
how easily the veneer is stripped away,
    how quickly the wolf can show up again
to remind us of how they've never
    been completely gone.

They strut around the property like new lords—
    loping along in the distance, tails vertical,
defiant, as if aware of the binoculars
    or veering close enough to give glares, teeth,
hackles to the yard dogs—

interested only in wolf things again,
    as if the partnership with humans
is just a bad memory,
    as if deep down everybody knows
that was all just an act to get fed.
    To hell with the cowardly ruse of being civil.
To hell with getting over in any way
    other than by growls or bared canines.

Two generations before, a dirt farmer worked
    cattle with their grandsire and dam, maybe
petted them once a week. Now the farmer's
    grandson wants to reach the 30-30
down from his truck rack,
    bring the window down slow,
and roll that part-shepherd/part-whatever

who's found his pack again
    and lives without qualm at pulling down
a newborn calf wet with placenta
    and ripping out its eyes.

Divorce Apartment Prayer

If it please, take this heaviness
clean away from me and my cat,
she who brightens at my crooked smile

and lives to glide beneath my palm,
for now we know in from out,
that muscle leads to ache,

that time is sometimes just a groan
in a cheap place off the highway,
that her chirping at sparrows

through bedroom window glass
will never be eating them.
Have felt the grip of Thy largesse

at the scruff of the neck;
Thy disposition, from above,
to impose on Thy creation

the bent hoot-owl beak of justice;
Thy tectonic will moving or paused,
cloud-like, season-sure,

out there in the white sunlight,
in the yard where court is held,
under the terrible paw of the day.

Dogged

Instinct says to hide what's unsaid
in tight smiles,

in turning away,

or, when what cousin Ray did to you
that summer you were seven is too much,

in a small box that doesn't even exist anymore,

full of memory that lost its memory
so as not to lose its mind.

Once made for King Edward Invincibles,
now packed with fear,

it's overflowing
with a decades-long tally
of tics around the mouth and eyes,
ghosts of skidmarked bedclothes,
jug tunes Oilcan Harry blew across the sphincter:

talismans that formative years conjured

and buried in old ground
so yellow pus would take decades
to swell the boil hidden in the psyche
to a throb.

***

Your self-accusing finger threatens   again,

turned back on itself,
then slithers like a borer worm

up your viscera,

intending to shut off the green light in the head.

***

Decades-old neglect
of the lot at the back of the past

       ensures a hard-packed,
              privet-bramble backyard
that's impervious to wishes' shovels,

         inscrutable as Daddy's face
until

     troubled adulthood hires a backhoe
         who has a notepad,
         an MSW,
         a calm manner.

What is found at first
    is a plastic Batman

      buried

      with a secret promise on his lips.

         Below that, nothing,
or close to it:
      something small,
         maybe a waft of rich loam.

***

In the new-cleared lot,
       what has for decades
passed for sentience

stops   for an instant.

          Rain begins,
    nostrils flare,

leaves turn up their lighter green sides.

The Need for a Grail

What do you say? That you're
here and ache for somewhere else, too,
somewhere you can't name,
only describe as like something? Maybe

like a stroll along a brick walk?
A jasmine-laced pergola ending at a smile?
Eyes that, looked into,
are more ice blue than periwinkle?

White mimosa, privet, delphinium,
sleep nectar, lavender,
cattail at dawn, memory of heaven,
hold-on-until-time-to-let-go?

No melting puddle
of want put into words
comes near cracking the window at 1 a.m.—
clear liquor of Alabama night,
cooldown of a June day—

and watching a black cat moonsheen,
her tiptoe from cedars,
her stop to slink down to sphinx
those few seconds
a night under stars turns holy,

her saunter toward morning,
reclaiming, as it happens she goes,
the scent of all the right near-misses:
of moving water, honeysuckle,
a newborn's skin, a raspberry-scented comet
up there speeding toward a place
where gold streets await the feet of souls.

Must Come Back

How selfless to martyr want
on the cross of renunciation.
Avoid Polaroids.

Otherwise, altruism won't abide.
One bodhisattva
per, please.

Why does being *real* or *good*
feel more like
being where you want to be?

Till the last hair's counted,
compulsion to seek a larger will
might will one to pledge

devotion to some Cause
Number One which/who has decided,
suitable paradox aplomb,

that failure to find the right here
is a given. Or anywhere else.
Even if heaven's in the head,

one must live a near miss
since the invisible
won't leave the tip of the tongue.

III

Grace/Indonesia

There's a reason
we must want to sit
in the dawn rain and drown

in the first light
near the small shed
down the path from the hill,
next to the boulder
people knew in their bones
before they knew
they were people.

We've got to
want to grow in fear and love
of the slow song
for our drowning selves,

in the just-intoned hum
of morning nearing as rain,
outcrop looming, big leaves
a giant's dripping fingers,

in a rooster's yelp so desperate
it cracks mid-crow,
like the thin, insucked
cry of a child
whose voice catches as she tries,
in tears, to explain herself.

In water blessing
lives lived in the gasp
before we let our drowning take us,
the rooster's plea
captures morning's earliest face
so well that we could die
for love of it,

the way we'll die to ourselves
in that watery roar,
for who we could've been
if we'd wanted it enough.

Whether Weather

Rain is
water drumming down
while drumming up sound
that calls rain to mind.

But an -ism doesn't drip,
leaf to white-oak leaf,
till a white oak is

so big it shades out thought.
What if the idea of water
ran along the tin roof,
then stair-stepped down?

Generous as a host
poor in fresh water
but ample in concern,

what if
sympathy
could quench reality's
long-suffered cottonmouth?

Forget or remember,
answer or look away,
this white oak's unfazed,

as heedless as it is big.
Construes nothing
but life
from the sky.

Purpose the Sky

A blanket of cricket whistle
and star drone shapes itself

over a mound of earth and stone.
One more humble ziggurat of grief.

Intentions have been caught and pinned,
as under a sleeping cat.

Guarded by night air,
half of Earth won't stop dreaming.

Without knowing, branches reach
into moonlight to feel for darkness.

An oak has grown itself tall, made a life,
rotted from the center.

When the castle of murmurs falls in,
what matters stands.

Shack Nap: May

Lightning turns ghosts
    back into shrubs and trees
when the sleeping mind is yanked
    across a pasture,

back to a waking place
    where cool air seeps
through a ragged window screen

    between a body that's probably mine
and eveningfall.
    My lips might be whispering,
"Cooling down."

    Thinking of dreaming,
dreaming of thinking.
    Cicadas still saw
away at the fading afternoon,

    but the serration's grown
half-hearted and slow
    since katydids came on.
Tree frogs burble and eeeee.

    Pewter ladle pours
a dark drink. I watch,
    through barely open slits,
swifts skywrite against cotton.

    Spring lightning has just lit. Again
I'm lying in the seconds
    before sound says how far,
in a house under cool sky

    after rain the color of air and water,
while cricket whistles
    slow the way back to now.

Wherewithal

Gotta think I got
more juice than you,
facts to the contrary.

Who cares? Not a fig.
Not insects making calls
shaped like fig leaves
same as in all the time
before thought
thought it had juice.

And all this
worry about one-upness
comes to not one
bullfrog about to jump.

Oaks, cicadas, sunsets:
shoulderless,
no chips.

That's how they
do the same thing
over and over
for the first time.

The Quality of Attention

All blue bugs are blue
    because they don't have to know
    who they are.
That goes for green, red, brown,
    yellow, and black, too,
    especially black because
    it's easier to become a world
    that makes you invisible at dusk.
Unlike humans, who are susceptible to bias,
    insects know without thinking
    that color is allegiance
    to the claw, juice, legs, carapace,
    and mouthparts of your subspecies.

Truth of identity translates to sound, too:
    noble chirruping in an instinct opera,
    arias peculiar to wind, leaf-rustle, tree frog,
    rapt proprioception of no-mind,
    no other thingness worthwhile
    in this moment, which anyway
    is all there is. Yes, Katy does.

Humans, though, can't stop
    banging their heads
    on the yellow
    cinderblock
    wall of consciousness.
The pain provokes relentless
    searching in the head,
    which shoves away all treasure.
Humans have no idea what they are,
    much less where or why,
    much less an authentic self to remember
    though they insist on believing otherwise.
Don't believe me?
    Look at the seconds ticking on your watch.
    Watch it as closely as you can
    for as long as you can.

The Postmodern

Davis had Monk on the session, a generosity
     few felt in those days toward the eccentric
     that critics said played like a slow child
     half-assing his weekly lesson. December of '54,
     Hackensack for Riverside.

Jackson was there, too, inveterately bop,
     all about the chops that solo turns
     in a tune like "The Man I Love"
     left rooms full of room to fill.

The leader of the session that was to be titled "Miles Davis
     and the Modern Jazz Giants," Davis blew his
     sad-little-boy horn through an adagio intro verse,
     followed by a break into double time,
     Jackson stepping out to mallet it in.
     A master at allusion and quotation,
     soloing for a full three minutes, he filled every measure
     with the cleverest of dense takes and one-ups
     of Hampton and Norvo, with apt homage
     to Ella and the Lady, hammering out
     every quick-witted phrase
     of a consummate veteran's backlog.

Finally, breathlessly, the tune still in double time,
     Jackson came to a gracious pause, leaving Monk an opening,
     which the Sufi master in sunglasses and *papakha*
     chose to fill with silence, dead livid living liquid air,
     a pocket of timelessness in time, a full ten seconds
     (which Davis would later say
     came from his asking Monk to lay out),

before very deliberately dropping a long, simple finger
     on the first note of the melody, backed only
     by Heath's pulse and the dry wash of Clarke's ride,
     then three seconds, the second note,
     then the wait and the third and fourth,
     plodding, plotting it out,
     as if he were just picking out a tune
     that had occurred to him instead of Gershwin,
     and it was being played for the first time.

Promise

*Only where there are graves
are there resurrections.*
                    —Nietzsche

Heartbeat spends itself on heartbeat,
the only buy it can get
in the only store in town.

Night, moon, Orion.
Though clouds try,
nothing can hide the show for long.

A pond says, "It's time,"
reflects,
insisting on up.

Seed
escapes into stasis:
the possible becomes possible.

Days are fire over tilled ground,
the earth so sweet its embrace may
just as well kill.

Long Time in the Wake

*Matter is an imaginary
and exploded substance.*
    —David Hume

Four little girls in an exploding church
            in Birmingham in September of 1963
were always already debris.

Already viscera and brains freed of sentience,
            already the fact of red-spattered print dresses
and young aspirations freed of bodies as if,
            by some decree,
girlish life, placid Sundays, and choir practice
            no longer made the picture complete.

As if, with dispatch, in past tense, in the philosophical realm,
            glass, cinder, wood, brick, and girl-flesh
had already imagined themselves in roaring pieces,
            paused, still flying along the alley to City Hall.

As if one could then stop-time the bang and come to see
            incendiary substance as instructive,
suspended in the crisp cool morning air
            and illustrating immutable laws.

The Bitter with the Sweet

The pink sheen of the numinous
markets itself as beyond the real,
but an apple grows from seed

in need more of manure than Significance.
Thanks to what ends up plowed under,
harvest proves itself on the tongue.

Coltrane's solos started growing before Monk,
before 1960 and quitting Miles to change jazz,
before LSD and Elvin,

before the windows in the universe flew open for him
and the notes became sheets of rain,
then lightning, then the sound

sound only approaches, as urgent and ineffable
as being unable to unsee a wind-whipped sky,
so deep blue it's terrifying,

beyond the black button eyes of a scarecrow;
as standing on the riverbank
and being unable to ignore, beneath your feet,

the underhum shudder of a passing barge;
as pretending to live under Jim Crow
when music was so much bigger than North Carolina.

Something was up that the man couldn't hide or hide from
about God being the music he couldn't escape,
so he played that out in the few years he had left,

but the tone of his horn always had a hardness,
an iron in it that would not go away,
like a hit you take to stay standing.

Grub for Delinquent

I prefer the unownable, gruff,
cotton-thick winter-coated
roguish cousin of the fox,
canine of independent bent
and unruly teeth, savvy,
relentless, risky wild pup
of the high yip.
Who's been known
to trip a jaw trap with a stick,
shit on it, and skip away.
Whom I seldom see
except for scat leavings
unless a spell overtakes a frozen afternoon
and the thicket shadow darkens
and there's a canter into a clearing
to check for cast-offs.
And who,
when I do step from the cabin
as quietly as boots allow
and see a dam and two pups
fifty yards upwind,
bring a heartbeat roar to my ear
and pride at having already offered
last night's leftover-bean homage
at the pasture's edge,
to those who've chosen,
muzzle up, soul steam escaping,
to be the cry in the dark.

To Stay in Etowah County

White cloud shadows ease over fat black buzzards
     lit on new-cut hay to scare off the chicken snake
     and yank away shreds of young rabbit
     mower blades have slung to pieces.

Wattled beaks grow blood-happy in the July spell:
     another summer's red tatters,
     another real mirage in a mown field by a river.

Coosa, we call it, conjuring our own stoop-shouldered Alabama,
     the heat-hissed, tobacco-spit names of the gone-before,
     by the fields where we grew withered sweating our own rivers,
     watching gabbling buzzards rip the guts out of opportunity.

In the woods by the now-fallow field,
     in the opening in the scrub tangle,
     in the privet-heavy shade, like a cemetery arisen,
     souls and their time on earth dapple
     and return, conjured to a forest theater of memory:

Dale, Sweetie, Gwen, Fat Roe, Benny
     burning off the cemetery so his daddy could die
     and so let the whiskey jaundice take him too,
     wall-eyed June with a Tareyton,
     Estelle at 90 bent down in the strawberries,
     slack-jawed Swann behind the feedstore counter,
     A. P. looking off the mountain at the L & N line
     following the valley between the ridges,
     Sarah looking past A. P.,

old Chief Turkey baffled at Forrest
     and the other crazy whites clanking by,
     Sullivan and his busted-up still,
     Woodrow with his Jim Beam to slow the Parkinson's,
     Jasmine, Rose, Basil, all people who are smells,

all peering through the heat blur past the edge of the field,
     from inside the shade submerged under the canopy
     of century-old oak, beech, poplar, from their place beyond,
     from a sweltering clearing where time is collapsed
     into the silenced hope it was meant to be,
     and the eyes you search for looking back are your own.

Acknowledgments

Thanks to the editors of the following journals for publishing many of these poems, some in other versions:

Aji: "Daddy's Bait"
Alexandria Quarterly: "History of the Absent"
The Aurorean: "Promise"
Broad River Review: "Readiness"
Change Seven: "Elvis Dives"
Concho River Review: "Instinct"
Cottonwood: "Athwart," "To the Task"
Faultline: "The Summer of My Father's 86th Year and My 56th"
Meat for Tea: "Dogged," "Grace/Indonesia," "Those Many Years"
October Hill: "Ishmael"
Pleiades: "Sami Painting"
Salt Hill: "Purpose the Sky"
Stoneboat: "The Ten Thousand Names of Dog"
West Texas Literary Review: "Whether Weather"

Thanks also to the family, friends, mentors, colleagues, fellow musicians, neighbors, and cats (my teachers all) who have remained constants in this slow learning curve. You know who you are.

Special thanks to Chris Lawson for being a good friend as well as an extraordinary artist and to Mike Dolinger for his superb execution of the cover design. You made my jumble of ideas into a book cover. Thanks also to Diane Kistner for being so kind and patient.

To those who help keep me reasonably sane: Jim and Tina Braziel, Richard Carlisle, Bob Collins, the Coosa Valley stalwarts, Ed Gartman, Asa and Jenny Gaston, Ted Haddin, Charlie Keener, Carol Van Laare, Richard and Nan Lawson, Hank Lazer and the Quiet Tide Sangha, Bill McKinney, Danny Siegel, Leslie Whatley, and Mike and Leslie Wingo.

And to those who've left us since: Phil Beidler, Clyde Blythe, Albert Butts, Richard Caples, Randa Graves, Jim MacIntosh, Allen Maxwell, Wanda McKinney, Alan Perlis, and Artis Waid.

About FutureCycle Press

FutureCycle Press is dedicated to publishing lasting English-language poetry in both print-on-demand and Kindle formats. Founded in 2007 by long-time independent editor/publishers and partners Diane Kistner and Robert S. King, the press was incorporated as a nonprofit in 2012. A number of our editors are distinguished poets and writers in their own right, and we have been actively involved in the small press movement going back to the early seventies.

Each year, we award the FutureCycle Poetry Book Prize and honorarium for the best original full-length volume of poetry we published that year. Introduced in 2013, proceeds from our Good Works projects are donated to charity. Our Selected Poems series highlights contemporary poets with a substantial body of work to their credit; with this series we strive to resurrect work that has had limited distribution and is now out of print.

We are dedicated to giving all of the authors we publish the care their work deserves, offering a catalog of the most diverse and distinguished work possible, and paying forward any earnings to fund more great books. All of our books are kept "alive" and available unless and until an author requests a title be taken out of print.

We've learned a few things about independent publishing over the years. We've also evolved a unique and resilient publishing model that allows us to focus mainly on vetting and preserving for posterity poetry collections of exceptional quality without becoming over-whelmed with bookkeeping and mailing, fundraising activities, or tax-ing editorial and production "bubbles." To find out more, come see us at futurecycle.org.

The FutureCycle Poetry Book Prize

All original, full-length poetry books published by FutureCycle Press in a given calendar year are considered for the annual FutureCycle Poetry Book Prize. This allows us to consider each submission on its own merits, outside of the context of a traditional contest. Too, the judges see the finished book, which will have benefitted from the beautiful book design and strong editorial gloss we are famous for.

The book ranked the best in judging is announced as the prize-winner in January of the subsequent year. There is no fixed monetary award; instead, the winning poet receives an honorarium of 20% of the total net royalties from all poetry books and chapbooks the press sold online in the year the winning book was published. The winner is also accorded the honor of being on the panel of judges for the next years competition; all judges receive copies of the contending books to keep for their personal library.

Made in the USA
Columbia, SC
17 December 2024

49129759R00043